FOREWORD

Welcome Reader, to a world of dreams.

For Young Writers' latest competition, we asked our writers to dig deep into their imagination and create a poem that paints a picture of what they dream of, whether it's a make-believe world full of wonder or their aspirations for the future.

The result is this collection of fantastic poetic verse that covers a whole host of different topics. Let your mind fly away with the fairies to explore the sweet joy of candy lands, join in with a game of fantasy football, or you may even catch a glimpse of a unicorn or another mythical creature. Beware though, because even dreamland has dark corners, so you may turn a page and walk into a nightmare!

Whereas the majority of our writers chose to stick to a free verse style, others gave themselves the challenge of other techniques such as acrostics and rhyming couplets. We also gave the writers the option to compose their ideas in a story, so watch out for those narrative pieces too!

Each piece in this collection shows the writers' dedication and imagination – we truly believe that seeing their work in print gives them a well-deserved boost of pride, and inspires them to keep writing, so we hope to see more of their work in the future!

Fragments Of Forever

Edited By Lynsey Evans

First published in Great Britain in 2024 by:

Young Writers
Remus House
Coltsfoot Drive
Peterborough
PE2 9BF
Telephone: 01733 890066
Website: www.youngwriters.co.uk

CONTENTS

Tilly Rorke (10)	60
Nia Joyner (7)	61
Sofia Bolton (9)	62
Elin Joyner (9)	63

Norwood Primary School, Peterborough

| Dayna Rogers (10) | 64 |
| Fola Akanbi (10) | 65 |

Oakley CE Junior School, Oakley

Sophie Richards (10)	66
Grace Smith (9)	67
Tess Clayton (9)	68
Zoya Naureen (9)	69
Beatrice Nevill (10)	70
Grace Minton (8)	71
Jessica Clacy (9)	72
Jack Meyer (9)	73
Heidi Day (7)	74
Matilda Varian (9)	75
Carah Morris (8)	76
Aislinn Hughes (9)	77
Fatoumata Binta Bah (11)	78
Leomi Lee-Buckland (8)	79
Rio Chan (9)	80
Lily Massey (8)	81
Holly Bennett (8)	82

Queen Elizabeth's Hospital School, Clifton

| Elliott Ginn (9) | 83 |

Sandbrook Community Primary School, Rochdale

Ariane Amaral (8)	84
Edie Warner (8)	85
Sumaiya Wasim (9)	86
Logan James Jones (8)	88
Esmae Boardman (8)	89
Olivia Speak (8)	90

Michelle Okpara (8)	91
Chioma Peace (9)	92
Hazel Lancaster (9)	93
Delphi Kershaw (8)	94
Excellent Ukpebor (9)	95
Habibah Mobeen (8)	96
Matilda Ida Pedley (9)	97
Aniya Ariana Habib (8)	98
Marwa Imran (9)	99
Haniya Aslam Rasheed (9)	100

St Anne's Catholic Primary School, Weeping Cross

Sreevidya Veeravalli (10)	101
Eva McGarrigle (10)	102
Pippa Hegarty (10)	104
Michelle Adedugbe (10)	106
Orla Byrne (9)	108
Rebecca Ashby (9)	110
Luke Harland (10)	112
Stephan Basson (10)	114
Ailen Colville (10)	115
Evelyn Markland (10)	116
Arthur Ferraz (10)	118
Max Dillon (10)	119
Sofia Salt (10)	120
Olivia Giannaki (10)	121
Jake Witkowski (10)	122
Sophia Lloyd (10)	123
Freddie Wallbank (9)	124
Raife Sims (9)	125
Zuzanna Rzaczkiewicz (10)	126
Angelin Juby (10)	127
Emilia Fletcher (9)	128
Ava Woolley (9)	129
Ethika Sangeeth (10)	130
Leo Fearns (10)	131
Nicole Kayibabu (10)	132
Yuvraj Singh Tiwana (10)	133
Sophie Thomas (10)	134
Jazz Ling (10)	135
Sophia Thompson-Attwooll (10)	136

Stakesby Primary Academey, Whitby

Zack Howard (11)	137
Elise Townshend (8)	138
Riley Leeman (8)	140
Emilie Newton (8)	141

Valley Primary School, Whitehaven

Layton Ferguson (10)	142
Bella Rose Plaskett (9)	144
Dunamis Obong (10)	146
Teddy Lynch (9)	148
Mabel Goode (9)	149
Millie Hanlon-Nixon (9)	150
Eva Hanlon-Nixon (9)	151
Lily Meldrum (9)	152
Ada McGregor (9)	153
Rory Hodgkiss (10)	154
Eve Wilkinson (9)	155
Oliver Bradshaw (10)	156
Felicity Rose Pearson (10)	157
Willow Hazelwood (10)	158
Tyler Cardy (9)	159
Evren Ozdemir (9)	160
Carlton Ennis (9)	161
Daven Mason (10)	162

Yohden Primary School, Peterlee

Jackson Ward (9)	163
Envy Devine	164
Layla Robinson (9)	165
Maya Hardy (9)	166
Ava Tanney (8)	167
Luka Lonsdale (9)	168
Ariyah Thomson (9)	169
Esmae Nixon	170
Layton Prince (9)	171
Freddie Anderson (9)	172
Isabella Peters (9)	173
Sadie Bell (9)	174

Sofia Bell May (9)	175
Thomas Wright (9)	176
Harley Storey (9)	177
Lily Wright (9)	178
Harvey Robson (9)	179
Ava Joan (8)	180

THE CREATIVE
WRITING

Dance To Your Heart

D ancing with friends, as happy as can be
A t the studio, that's where I feel free
N ever forget to point your toes and smile
C reating routines can take a long while
E llie, Delilah and Zoe, all like performing

T ap dancing is my favourite, not at all boring
O ut on the stage, the lights are so bright

Y ou can see the people, but that's all right
O ne, two, three, four, five, six, seven, eight
U nderstanding timing can make it look great
R eady and waiting for the judge to rise

H appy to hear I've won first prize
E veryone is clapping as loud as they can
A n amazing feeling, that they are my fan
R ight at the front, my family are sitting
T ears in their eyes, but Nana is knitting!

Sophie Bird (10)
Barlestone CE Primary School, Barlestone

The Snowy Night Wolf

One little boy called Ben lived in America. His parents decided to move to Antarctica. When his parents told Ben he was sad to hear he was leaving his home country.

On Monday at 11am they left to catch the plane. It took three days to get to Antarctica. When they got there it was 12pm. Ben was tired and went to bed.

The next day Ben went to explore for a few minutes. It was silent but he heard her howl. He went to see what it was. It was a wolf. It had white and black fur and her eyes were different colours, one was sky blue and the other emerald green. He looked up, what an animal it was. It was a snowy night wolf.

Ben wanted to keep it, so he asked his mum and she said yes, so he called her Skye. But little did he know the snowy night wolf would save the world.

Jason Barber (10)
Barlestone CE Primary School, Barlestone

Mythology

Through the sea,
Live the pirates and me,
We travel past mermaids and seals,
Past gulls, sirens and eels,
As we land on the coast,
We all make the most,
Of the food we have on board,
When we look south,
We see the mouth of a fiery dragon,
When we look north,
We see a horse beside an old wagon,
The wagon is filled to the brim with treasure,
Which gives me and the pirates great pleasure,
But in our way,
To my dismay,
Is a Cyclops with dreadlocks.
Then he set us on a chase,
And he tried to hit us with a mace,
Then he finally spoke,
I didn't hear what he said because then I awoke.

Albert Clooney (10)
Barlestone CE Primary School, Barlestone

Teal Treasure

I walk all alone,
In a forest,
I love it.
Sunrise coming up.
Suddenly, a loud crack.
I stop in my tracks.
Saucer eyes getting rounder,
A rock splits open - *crack!*
A scaly head pops out.
Its teal scales glimmer prettily,
The dragon yowls happily.
He loves me, I love him.
We play together,
Swim together,
Have fun together.
Sun is setting,
Its golden glow again.
Goodbye, dear dragon.
I'll see your
Teal scales
Again.

Georgie Ashton (10)
Barlestone CE Primary School, Barlestone

Wonders Of The Forest

One day I got trapped in a forest,
My sister was trying to find me,
But I was nowhere to be seen!
But what's that?
My stomach is turning and I'm all alone,
What can I do now?
Something appears in front of me,
It's a dragon,
I run, I'm scared, it follows me.
What does it want?
It's by my side, it sings,
It wants to play,
We play tag and a long game of fetch,
But it is time to say our goodbyes,
We went home,
It's over.

Zoe Bartlam (10)
Barlestone CE Primary School, Barlestone

The Tide

Once upon a time in a land far away,
I dreamt of the tide coming in and out every single day.
The sun would shine high in the sky,
Whilst the birds would fly up high.
Mermaids sat in the blue lagoon,
I was sad to leave here so soon,
But when I opened my eyes,
All I could see was the moon.
Back in my bed, sleeping at home,
This was a dream I would never let go.

Lilly Tisor (10)
Barlestone CE Primary School, Barlestone

Dance Nightmare

Once upon a dream,
I was in the dressing room,
Waiting for my group to dance.
We got called and went on stage.
In the middle of the dance,
I heard a crack, but nobody else heard.
Just then, a big orange flame blew up,
And the alarm went off.
We evacuated the theatre,
And then I opened my eyes,
And I was in my comfortable bed,
Safe in my house.

Bella Griffiths (10)
Barlestone CE Primary School, Barlestone

Adventures

Woke up this morning, got out of bed.
Heard a funny noise and a tingling in my head.
Opened a window and looked outside.
A festival of fun, trying to hide.
Looked around, opened the door.
And to my surprise, there was so much more!
Round and round, a merry-go-round.
A roller coaster zoomed up from the ground.
And there I was standing in awe.
Because of the things that I just saw.

Later that evening, I had a funny feeling.
It was like a warm, cosy hug.
I went outside and saw a hole that someone must have dug.
But it was really small!
Probably the smallest of them all!
I turned around and heard a noise!
But nothing was there! No girls and no boys.
I saw something, there it was.
A little kitten from up above.
Super cute and light like a pillow,
She was a bit white with some yellow!

She took me on adventures
And across the seven seas,
Everywhere we went, no one caught a disease!

Scarlett Hurson (9)
Bush Primary School And Nursery Unit, Dungannon

Alien Invasion

I n a special concealed concert just in case of a thunderstorm, little do fans know, it's more than that.

N ations go crazy as aliens disembark in Antarctica - the world is going crazy. In the South West, more emerge.

V ictims in the streets, aliens' fights come to a halt as American Marines run them over in armoured tanks.

A merica's victims may have a problem but it is worse in Moscow - the president takes action.

"S orry," says Germany, "I have no guns." America replies, "We don't care. Fight."

I n an instant, Iceland is hit. Aliens disembark; fighting takes place and it's war.

"O nwards!" sergeants shout. "Fight them now!"

N ormandy is won - not taken by Germany (that's for sure). It's even worse in the other nations.

Harry Swann (9)

Bush Primary School And Nursery Unit, Dungannon

Talking Footballs

"**F** or the longest time of my life, I'm stuck in this stupid castle room."

O h my goodness, is a football talking to me? The football said, "I know how you get out of this place!"

"**O** kay, hurry up and tell me so I can become a professional footballer."

T his talking football thinks it knows me, really? And why is it my favourite football?

B ut he said, "The only way you're going to get out of this place is if you puncture me."

A ll my life, I've had my favourite football and I have to puncture it!

L aughing, "Really, do you know I have to puncture you?" "So do it." "Fine, I've done it."

"**L** ook," then I ran onto the pitch and became a professional footballer.

Chloe Bell (8)
Bush Primary School And Nursery Unit, Dungannon

A Trip To The Moon

We're going on a trip to the moon,
And we're going to get there very soon,
Of course, everybody was jumping about,
Like a bunch of bouncing balloons.

Then came the day,
We all shouted hip-hip-hooray!
We went to a place where the rockets take off,
It was near the sea that frolicked and frothed,
Then we got in and at last, we took off!
We zoomed past galaxies, planets and moons,
We looked behind the bars,
As we shot past the stars,
At last, as we landed, we saw something strange,
It was a massive collision and range,
Of aliens all shapes and size,
And all of a sudden they began to rise.

Then I closed and opened my eyes and realised,
I was in my bed,
Safe and sound cuddling my Ted.

Anna Montgomery (9)
Bush Primary School And Nursery Unit, Dungannon

The Premiership Dream

Linfield beating The Swifts 1-0 in the 88th minute
The Swifts equalised and the crowd goes wild
The pitch as damp as a rainforest
I can smell smoke from flares
The stadium as crowded as a concert

The Swifts on the attack
The keeper makes a great save
Noise is clamorous
Drums beating loudly

Corner comes in
Dean Curry, the captain, headers it
It goes in!
The ball goes smash into the net

I can see flares being lit
The stands' screams erupt in the stadium
Players hop into celebration with the fans
Linfield in shock

Full-time whistle goes
Pitch invasion as The Swifts stay up
Portadown gets relegated.

Charlie Robinson (9)
Bush Primary School And Nursery Unit, Dungannon

A 3am Fright!

One day, I was in school,
It was as cold as a pool,
Then my teacher said we were going on a trip,
So I dropped my biro tip.

So then I sprang out of my chair,
When she said it was a funfair,
I had so much joy!
Like a five-year-old boy getting a toy.

On the day,
All I could do was pray!
I saw a toad.

When we got there it was scary,
Like Bloody Mary!
The rides were bad,
They made me sad.

Time for a nap
The last thing I heard was *tap!*
I was woken at midnight by a *click!*

I saw a clown!
I closed my eyes...
But never woke up!

After two days, I lay awake,
I saw a cake,
I realised it was all a dream!

Jessica Smyth (9)
Bush Primary School And Nursery Unit, Dungannon

A Candy World

Oreos eat gummy bears,
Rolos swim and drink.
Volcanoes laugh at lollipops,
As their sticks all sink.

Trot-trot goes the Pegasus,
Whoosh goes her white wings.
Pop went the sugar balloons,
"Lah!" the sweet birds sing.

Scent of chocolate fills the air,
Hear the chocolate birds.
Taste the sweet cotton candy,
See the fluffy herds.

Colours bright like art palettes,
Fill the lovely sky.
Sherbet as magical as fairy dust,
Makes you soar so high.

Fluffy puppies all around,
Rides of all colours.
Joyful freedom, hear the sound,
Jump and scream, "Hooray!"

Rayna Cummings (9)
Bush Primary School And Nursery Unit, Dungannon

The Football World

F inally I found my football in the hedge, but when I picked it up it jumped out of my hands and down the road, far away.

O ut of nowhere, Mbappé ran after the ball, caught it and brought it back to me.

"O utstanding performance today," said Mbappé as he walked off, but I followed him.

"T oday I scored a hat-trick for PSG," said Mbappé.

B radley scored his first goal for Liverpool.

A nd out of nowhere, Mo Salah went and scored, top corner, versus Chelsea.

L iverpool won the league in 2018

L iverpool won the Champions League in 2019.

Oliver Newell (9)
Bush Primary School And Nursery Unit, Dungannon

Nightmares

N ightmares come to life and it gives me a fright

I t is dark and monsters are prowling in sight

G ives me shivers down my spine as the monsters wander around

H ands of phantoms grab and grasp but do not make a sound

T he glass shatters as they come into the house

M y knees wobble, scared as a mouse

A s the buildings fall, the monsters still call

R oar! I go to a dinosaur as I see a ball

E veryone runs as the monsters chase the people down

S mile on my face because it was all a dream.

Denis Arhipovs (9)
Bush Primary School And Nursery Unit, Dungannon

Candy Land

C ake being baked, smelling delicious,

A nd touching juicy watermelon there.

N owhere else is as sweet as here.

D own the stairs I go – weird things happen,

Y ellow dresses swinging around. "What are you doing?" They didn't answer.

L ots of pants magically appear - one even got married,

A nd hats fly around me singing Happy Birthday.

N oodles fighting like always,

D affodils chatting like usual.

And this is my Candy Land.

Geovanna De Sousa (9)
Bush Primary School And Nursery Unit, Dungannon

Jumping Clouds

C ome along up to the clouds and start jumping.

L oud noises are up there – It sounds like lots of fun.

O ut there in the bright distance, go and see all the beautiful animals up in the trees.

U nder the sea, there are lots of sea animals. They even jump up in the air and do lots of fun tricks.

D ogs jump high as trees up in the sky, as you can see. It sounds like lots and lots of fun.

S ome baby monkeys are out there too. It will be great to go and see what they are up to.

Louise Parr (9)
Bush Primary School And Nursery Unit, Dungannon

Don't Run

The children's screaming becomes louder
I'm running towards the mansion,
I feel fear as I get closer
I look behind me, there is a doll,
Scared most of all,
Getting close, terrified,
Running like a maniac
The doll floating towards me,
Whoever is watching, this is a goodbye.

Somehow I survived,
Running for my life as the doll comes towards me...
I'm terrified.

...Wait, was this all a dream?

Franklin Irwin (9)
Bush Primary School And Nursery Unit, Dungannon

Pet Party

As you walked in, to your delight,
You saw a puppy in the light.
All cute and fluffy, calling, "Tickle me!"
Dancing happily and playfully.
You took a few steps in and... whoa!
A bunny - her eyes with a glow.
I felt the silkiness of her fur,
Then heard a sudden purr.
Once I was fully in, I jumped with glee,
I went to my friend, her surname with a 'C'.
Me and you were meant to be,
Just you wait and see.

Darcey Cummings (9)
Bush Primary School And Nursery Unit, Dungannon

Bunny's Marshmallow

On Saturday morning, I wake up,
And see millions of little pups.
I go through my candy portal,
And there I turn human to immortal.
As I slide along,
I sing my favourite song!
Whoosh! I go down the slide,
Now I'm at Candy World!
As Bunny jumps on me,
The emergency bell rings.
Marshmallow volcano explodes,
While Bunny laughs with glee.
I pick a pink and magical marshmallow,
Just for Bunny and me!

Isabella Hogg (9)
Bush Primary School And Nursery Unit, Dungannon

Island Of Evil

The storm howled in the night,
The water was as cold as ice.
The old shack moaned in the wind.

My skin is made of wax,
My eyes are seashells,
My hair is made of seaweed.

My friend is a werewolf.
My pet is a ghost dog.

The three witches brew in the old shack,
Making poison to test on children.

The sea smashed against the rock.

The ghouls eat the fear of humans.
I am stuck here forever.

Alex McLernon (9)
Bush Primary School And Nursery Unit, Dungannon

Living Among The Dinosaurs

It all started when dinosaurs were alive.
We went back in time.
We saw trees, bushes and pterodactyls, as well as raptors and a T-rex chasing raptors.
But the T-rex smelled us.
And it chased us.
We ran as fast as we could!
Then we came across a spinosaurus.
It ran towards us. We ran again, but the T-rex caught up.
They started fighting, but the T-rex won the fight.
It roared so loud that we had to cover our ears.

Tommy McCartney (9)
Bush Primary School And Nursery Unit, Dungannon

Winnie The Pooh

When I woke up in the morning
I had a big fright
Now I needed to get home
I didn't want to miss school

You need to look at the sign
Time for a big surprise
Winnie stood in front of me

"Hello," Winnie said to me
With every step, I got closer to him
Piglet had come to play on this day
On this day, Tigger came to play
Ordinary days are fun but this was the best.

Ellie-May Dowzell (9)
Bush Primary School And Nursery Unit, Dungannon

Puppies Can Do Gymnastics

P uppies like to play all day long.
U nfortunately, I can't lift the dogs, but they can lift me.
P uppy power, and they have all types.
P uppies like puppaccinos because they are lovely.
I love all types, I think they're bright.
E xciting day of my life – a new puppy!
S ome know how to do gymnastics, and some don't, but I will teach them.

Sophie Parr (9)
Bush Primary School And Nursery Unit, Dungannon

Tiger Pop

T here were lots and lots of bushes, my word there were lots,

I turned my head and *pop*, what was that?

G osh, what a fright it was. I thought, *what was that?*

E agerly I turned my head because the pop went again and again,

R unning away over bushes and flowers,

S illy me, it was my best friend - Stripes!

Anna Cummings (9)

Bush Primary School And Nursery Unit, Dungannon

Nightmare

N ight has come
I n the deep, dark woods
G oing deeper into the darkness
H eart pounding at the moonlight
T rembling knees
M akes me sneeze
A re you over there?
R eady to run into the sun
E ventually out.

Sam Sinnamon (9)
Bush Primary School And Nursery Unit, Dungannon

The Horse Which Ran Away Today

A horse ran away today
To get some hay
He ate and ate all day long

Following him quickly
I galloped off with his friend
Then he gave me a kick

A flick of his mane
Never looked the same again
Until the dame brushed his mane.

Jessica Edwards (9)
Bush Primary School And Nursery Unit, Dungannon

Best Day Ever Dream

D ancing, walking to the swimming pool
R eady to feel the cold water on my fingers
E veryone is ready to slide down the slide
A fter me, my best friend is ready to slide
M y best friend is ready to walk to the park.

Medeina Venclovaite (9)
Bush Primary School And Nursery Unit, Dungannon

Football Dreams

D oing penalty kicks for Manchester United.

R aging because our team lost.

E xcited crowd.

A fter the first half, score 2-1.

M any people in the crowd.

S tart of the second half.

Luke Kirk (9)
Bush Primary School And Nursery Unit, Dungannon

Into Space In My Dream

Once upon a dream, a dream came true,
It was a dream with me and you.
I wished upon a little star,
It shot off so very far,
Into the solar system, up, up high,
And in my dream, I started to fly.

I flew with all the owls at night,
The view was so beautiful, what a sight.
But suddenly, I started to fall until something caught me,
It was an alien family.
They carried me up on their alien ride,
I was amazed and so surprised!

They carried me up into space,
It was a strange sort of place.
They took me up through the universe,
Their ride started wobbling, I thought it was cursed.
But suddenly there was a *bang*,
I had got back in bed with all of my gang.

Ava Osborne (9)
Etz Chaim Jewish Primary School, Mill Hill

The Greatest Singer

There she is, up on the stage,
Is she going to win the game?
Hey, it's me – the greatest singer
And do you want to see me dance?
Then watch me.

Is she going to win the game?
Is she? Is she?
Argh! She won the game!
Mila Okret, please come up
And here's your ticket to
Italy! Woo-hoo!

I'm on the plane to Italy
And I'm going to win the game
I can see the lights
For the Eurovision.

Five minutes later, I'm
Here and
It is now
I can't believe it! Argh!

Now it's my turn
Can I do this? Yes, I can!
Woo! Yeah! The winner is...
Mila Okret!

Mila Okret (8)
Etz Chaim Jewish Primary School, Mill Hill

Curiosity Of Outer Space

Once upon a dream, I saw,
Planets, stars, rockets, more,
The curiosity in my head,
All just happening in my bed.

I had jumped really high,
Almost like I could fly,
I went to explore,
You won't believe what I saw.

Rockets, shooting stars,
Space rocks, even Mars,
The great colours I could find,
All just happening in my mind.

Suddenly, it got all dark,
I could not find a single spark,
I knew if I saw no supernova,
That my dream was sadly over.

Gracie Carr (9)
Etz Chaim Jewish Primary School, Mill Hill

My Dream Is Over

M ist all around, nowhere to go
Y ou've probably never heard of...

D arkness all around
R unning away. Oh no! I can't get out
E vening falls,
A nd it's even darker than before
M y dream is over. Goodbye, I'll see you soon.

I 'm back
S omehow

O ver there
V ictorious, I call him
E verywhere
R ound. Now, I'm really going. Goodbye. I mean it!

Shulamit Brown (8)
Etz Chaim Jewish Primary School, Mill Hill

A Land Of Dreams

Just think about a shooting star,
Or a big chocolate bar!

Once upon a wish,
I lie in bed,
And these thoughts swell in my head,
Land of dreams, land of wishes,
Created by a loud *swish!*

I toss and turn,
I hear a loud groan.
Something is chasing me,
I run. I try to flee.
I open an eye,
And hear my clock going *tick-tock*,
I am at home,
Happily there is no one chasing me!
Hopefully...
Dreams could be anything!

Madeline Wolfin (9)
Etz Chaim Jewish Primary School, Mill Hill

Playing In Goal

I once dreamt I was in goal,
Saving shots from pole to pole.

In the World Cup, I played well,
All the way until the bell.

In the semis, it was hard,
But I acted like a guard.

After that, it went to pens,
But I saved from many ends.

My team had the final shot,
And the ball looked like a dot.

It was finally time,
The World Cup trophy would be mine!

Ezra Kotkis (9)
Etz Chaim Jewish Primary School, Mill Hill

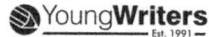
Football

I dream of football.
I dream of being a famous player.
I dream of scoring in a match.
I dream of being a captain in a team.
I dream of having new boots.
I dream of winning the Champions League.

Tommy Guz (9)
Etz Chaim Jewish Primary School, Mill Hill

Monster In Me!

I can see something waiting for me, a soul sleeping
within my reach, but that soul is my very own!
I am all alone, with no one here for me, they're all in
their coffins, locked in tight!
I'm in a basement all alone, except, the monster in
myself.
I now feel sad, scared, petrified and hurt because my
head, arm, ear and nose are bleeding!
I finally see the monster that was in myself, whenever
the monster is in pain I'm in pain!
Then, the monster leaves...
And then he goes in someone else,
Now I'm free!

Bonnie Leigh Jenkins (9)
Llangynwyd Primary School, Llangynwyd

The Wizard Book

I can see a wizard in my dream,
A fun nice wizard had a pet lizard,
The rainbow lizard loves to play almost every day,
The lizard's favourite thing to do is play.

I feel amazing and outstanding,
Famous fairies flying away in the shining sky.

I see royal pirates getting lost in space,
I am with a pirate that's loud and proud,
Fairyland is sparkling, lots of people are running.

Lexi Sutton (9)
Llangynwyd Primary School, Llangynwyd

Magical Creatures

I can see unicorns and dinosaurs and wizards and fairies.
My friend, he has black hair and he is happy all the time and he likes to rhyme.
I feel excited and happy, the happiest I've ever been.
In Dreamworld, it's colourful and sweet and he swept me off my feet and I could see the starlight.
A unicorn picked me up and we swept through the air and it was magical.

Amelia Reed (8)
Llangynwyd Primary School, Llangynwyd

The Weird Wizard

I see a magical jungle in front of my eyes
And I am excited for the sunrise inside
And I feel like I'm shining, I'm walking in
And I feel like a weird wizard is watching
But not the wizard on Royalty Green.

My friend is being weird
She got a dragon-style dress
It scares me a bit
I feel okay but like someone is watching me
Through the trees and leaves.

Khloe Coleman (9)
Llangynwyd Primary School, Llangynwyd

Sea Of Treats

I could see a land of treats which greeted me.
At least I had my shiny horse.
But I was in a forest of sweets and treats.
I was terrified and enlightened,
Nervous, above all.
I climbed and crawled under rocks,
And stones big and small and round.
In a while, I found some food, and got rescued,
And I lived happily ever after.

Evan Thomas (8)
Llangynwyd Primary School, Llangynwyd

A Night In The Magic Cave

Me, my friend and also my brother woke up in the middle of the night. Me, my friend and my brother went to Spain where we found red and pink lucky huskies. We petted them. They were soft, fluffy and scruffy. Then we saw a wizard lizard husky that shimmered. White fairies appeared, then the night ended and we went home.

Luna Thomas (8)
Llangynwyd Primary School, Llangynwyd

The Circus

I felt something was waiting for me and then I got trapped. And then I saw I was in a circus. I saw clowns and animals. It was frightening and scary.
I was with two friends, Allie and Elijah. We were getting surrounded by clowns. I was put in a car and I never saw my friends again. I wasn't fed for seven days.

Zac Henderson (8)
Llangynwyd Primary School, Llangynwyd

The Wizard's Magic

I was in a building very old, I felt cold,
The wizard turned himself into a brick, showing
everyone a trick,
The magical place looked like a purple light room with
lots of potions,
He did another magic trick to make me fly,
And that wizard turned himself into a lizard.

Aidan Rosser (7)
Llangynwyd Primary School, Llangynwyd

Pirates

Pirates staring at me from afar,
Pirates staring at me from a car.
Feeling like a star,
Waiting for a spar.
I am going to find Qatar,
And I am going to find a cool car.
To go and see the pirates,
And wave coolly like some tea.

Ivy Parfitt (8)
Llangynwyd Primary School, Llangynwyd

Me In My School

I was in my school, which was boring, and I was learning something new.
When I got to math, I started to laugh, but when I started, I farted.
After that, all my mates faded, and only the shadow stayed.
The monster came out of the ground and killed me.

Matthew Boldenko (9)
Llangynwyd Primary School, Llangynwyd

Me In New York

I can see the Empire State Building
It's very tall, I feel very small
Random people wearing suits
I am eating fruit
I am on the Metro to work
I am in a luxurious hotel
In the pool
I feel really cool.

Antony Davies (9)
Llangynwyd Primary School, Llangynwyd

My Dog Dottie And Our Friends

As I am staring out of my bedroom window,
With Dinky Dottie, I look out at the beautiful spring meadow.

I say to Dottie, "Shall we go for a walk?"
Dinky Dottie, the talking doggie, says, "I'm too tired to even talk."

So instead, we get cosy and watch some cartoons on the telly,
We curl up with our blankets, and we munch on popcorn and jelly.

In the morning, we are up bright and early,
Ready to go to the flowery spring meadow and find a magical stone that is pearly.

In the spring sun, the swaying trees,
The change of season comes with a steady breeze.

Then who do we see?
But my fantastic best friend, Penelope!

We are both walking our faithful dogs,
Running through the woods and jumping over mossy logs.

We are having so much fun,
We forget all about our healthy lunch.

Watching the blossoms from the trees fall,
Penelope spots a pearly ball!

We follow this ball that rolls with the wind,
We look at each other with our huge, big grins.

Our dogs are running free,
We hide behind the trees.

Then we look up, and, oh no!
We're lost, and we don't know where to go.

Dottie looks up and tells us not to worry,
"I'll get us home! We'll be there shortly!"

Dottie sniffs with her shiny black nose,
Weaving back and forth and away, she goes.

Before we know it, we are home safe and sound,
I'm sure glad Dottie is here to lead us homeward
bound.

Jessica Taylor (8)
Newton Poppleford Primary School, Newton Poppleford

A Deadly Dream

At night when I'm curled up in my bed,
Thoughts of monsters fill my head.
Some are enormous, some are small,
Some are stumpy, and some are tall.
Some are red, and some are blue,
Some have three eyes instead of two.
This one's pink, and this one's yellow,
And at night they all say, *"Hello!"*
But they are not a friend,
Meeting them could be your end.
Their teeth are as sharp as a pizza slicer,
If they were blunter it would definitely be nicer!
I am lying there in my bed as scared as can be,
And suddenly, suddenly, dreams take hold of me.
Along the grass I am strolling,
Over the hills that are rolling.
There are beautiful flowers, and tall lean trees,
And sometimes I see colourful buzzing bees.
Oh and what's that? Is it a snake?
I am unaware of the food I will make!
It wraps round my foot and crawls up my leg,
And holds me down like a helpless peg.
It twists up my body and up to my head,

And I think this may even be my deathbed.
Then I think, *what could it be holding me tight?*
It's a snaking tree root with great might!
It lifts me up and, "Aah! It's a tree with a mouth!"
Now my life is really going south!
The gaping jaws are sucking me in,
My patience with this place is wearing thin.
What a monstrous land this is, I think,
Then I wake up with a sudden blink.

Harlan Ireland (9)
Newton Poppleford Primary School, Newton Poppleford

Untitled

I open my eyes and what do I see
Floating music like oceans and sea.
As I look in the distance, I can see,
A tall glowing figure smiling at me.
And in a flash, she disappears.
I chase and I chase without endless tears.
Rushing through my dreams,
I soon feel like all badness has fled.
From bouncing bunnies to racing horses
I know this is all a part of me.
Soon, the dream of flying reaches me,
I'm up so high but then I wonder...
What light lies beneath those hopeful wings?
Then everything goes dark, dead trees and empty
caves.
I hear a whine and a bark.
A dog that cries.
Ash runs down his leg.
But as I touch, brightness shines.
My nightmare is gone in and out.

Amity Day-Kerry (9)
Newton Poppleford Primary School, Newton Poppleford

Dreams

The land of dreams, a place of wonder and delight,
Where reality fades into the night,
Visions dance before my eyes,
As I wander under starlit skies.

In this realm of fantasy and imagination,
I am free from the constraints of limitations,
I can fly with the wings of a bird,
Or swim with creatures of the sea, unheard.

The colours are brighter, sounds more clear,
In the place where all my dreams appear,
I can be whoever I want to be,
And the vastness of my creativity.

But as the morning light begins to creep,
I know it's time to wake from my sleep,
Back to the world of responsibilities and chores
But I'll carry with me all the magic of these dreams.

Edie Craddock (9)
Newton Poppleford Primary School, Newton Poppleford

A Moonlit Dance

Moonlight gives off a beautiful shimmer
As fairies begin to dance.
Dragons breathe fiery flames
As they twirl and prance.

Wizards and witches come together
To join this festive scene.
Magic fizzles in the air and ground
As colourful as any dream.

Writers and athletes, teachers and dancers
Come and work together.
With bonds of friendship so strong
It will last forever.

Royalty arrives at the party
Bowed into the gates.
They clap, sing and dance
And celebrate.

And so this magical time
Is filled with laughter and treats.

Such a spectacular thing
That everyone desires to meet.

This is how a dream should be.

Wren Hibbett (9)
Newton Poppleford Primary School, Newton Poppleford

Lamplight

Up ahead,
Through the clouds,
I see the lamplight glow.
It guides me through the darkness,
It shows me where to go.

Suddenly, it disappears,
I shout out for help.
And out of nowhere,
Something leads me,
Through the dark of the night.

It saved my life.
It saved my soul.
And now we're in the daylight,
But my saviour's disappeared.

I wonder who it was that night,
But I guess I'll never know.
Oh well, it doesn't matter now,
It turns out it was all,
A dream!

Tilly Rorke (10)
Newton Poppleford Primary School, Newton Poppleford

What Dreams Mean To Me

We all dream dreams,
Some scary,
Some frightful,
Some happy,
Some delightful,
What dreams mean to me.

We all have different dreams,
Some with fairies,
Some with wizards,
Some with pirates,
Some with lizards,
What dreams mean to me.

Where dreams take you,
To the Amazon rainforest,
To Disneyland,
To the Sahara Desert,
To the beach playing in the sand.

What dreams mean to me,
What do dreams mean to you?

Nia Joyner (7)
Newton Poppleford Primary School, Newton Poppleford

The Moon Stone

The burns
The scratches
Shredded to pieces
As they went
Bang tap went the rats
They went
Tunnel to tunnel
Through the mysterious dark
They pushed and pushed
Through the trench of blood
Into the glowing moon sky
There it was
The glistening rock
Known as
The Moon Stone
Then I woke up.

Sofia Bolton (9)
Newton Poppleford Primary School, Newton Poppleford

Dreams

I opened my eyes
I couldn't believe what I saw
A forest beyond my imagination
A vast open stretch of sand
Water rushing past my face
A winter wonderland
Then, suddenly, I fell
Down...
Down...
Down...
Through all reality.
I opened my eyes,
It was all over.

Elin Joyner (9)
Newton Poppleford Primary School, Newton Poppleford

Sport Is The Best

Sport is the best,
I dream about it every night,
My football team winning a match,
When I catch the ball in netball,
Oh no! I clashed with the goalkeeper!
Oh, I get so eager when I score a goal,
Eww! My really old shoe has mould!
I sold my old ball so I can get a new one!
I get very sad when the match is done,
I get mad when the referee pulls me off,
I hate when I wake up from my dreams, because I am
late for breakfast!
My friend, Kate, loves to hear about my dreams,
She tells me she loves them more than her favourite
song!

I am sorry this poem is not the best,
It is my bedtime and I want to dream about rounders
or football or netball,
I want to dream about something else...
Just kidding!
They're probably like the rest!

Dayna Rogers (10)
Norwood Primary School, Peterborough

A Funny Thing

Dreams, dreams
They can be funny little things
Or funny big things

They can be happy
They can be sad
They can be good
Or they can be bad

You should cherish the happy ones
And cancel out the scrappy ones.

Fola Akanbi (10)
Norwood Primary School, Peterborough

Sweet Dreams

S oaring above the clouds with me are rainbow Pegasus.

"W ow!" I say as I look all around at the gorgeous, big, blue sky.

E verywhere I look are bright, fluffy clouds,

E ach one of them plump and white like daisies.

T he sweetest of dreams are always the happiest.

D reamy clouds above a beautiful sunrise.

R oaming around with me, a pretty Pegasus.

E very step like walking on soft, squishy marshmallows.

A sleep the whole time, yet it feels so real.

M oments after the golden sunrises, I lose focus in my dream.

S uddenly I wake up, clueless of the night before.

Sophie Richards (10)
Oakley CE Junior School, Oakley

Unicorns

U nimaginably, a unicorn, my eyes I can see

N ervously, I step forward and say, "Hello, would you be a dear and get me a tea?"

I n response, the unicorn says, "My name is Violet. I don't have any tea but you could do some fun activities with me."

"C ertainly, will you be my best friend? It would really please me."

"O bviously, you're the best!"

"R avishing, let's go and get started!"

N ow, the day is getting late. We have played all of our games and now we're off to bed

S uddenly, I am in my room. It was all a dream.

Grace Smith (9)
Oakley CE Junior School, Oakley

The Impossible Dream!

Some dreams are not impossible like...
Being famous, a footballer or a dancer!
Being a teacher, a clown or a builder!
Being an astronaut or not being afraid of spiders
You could be a writer or an athlete maybe

Some dreams are impossible like...
Being a wizard or having superpowers!
Seeing a pirate or maybe some fairies!
Flying around or you could be royalty!
You might get lost or see a fire-breathing dragon!
You could ride a unicorn or maybe a huge and scary dinosaur
Or just see monsters under the bed

My dream is for the world to be Minecraft
Or to have my own game like Roblox.

Tess Clayton (9)
Oakley CE Junior School, Oakley

Coming To Earth

A normal girl minding her own business. All was going well until one fateful afternoon, she heard a noise in her garden. Wondering what it was, Ellie hurried outside to peek. With shock on her face, she thought, *what's this?*

In the middle of her garden was a spaceship! Fragilely opening it up, she was in fright. Inside was an alien. "Please don't hurt me," pleaded Ellie. But soon she realised it was as scared of her as she was of it.

"I'm sorry," whispered the alien. "I led them here."

"Who?"

"Them!"

Coming in the distance were spaceships...

Zoya Naureen (9)
Oakley CE Junior School, Oakley

Like An Eagle, I Fly

In my dreams every night,
My imagination starts to ignite.
The picturesque mountains stand so tall,
And up above them, I feel so small.
Like an eagle, I fly,
Up into the azure-blue sky.
I soar through the clouds, which look like cotton candy,
and continue my journey, turning this way and that,
It's so amazing and exhilarating and that is a fact!
Every time I start to fly,
Iridescent unicorns come and say hi.
But every time I have to go,
They say goodbye really slow.
Suddenly my imagination goes to sleep,
And the adventures are for me to keep.

Beatrice Nevill (10)
Oakley CE Junior School, Oakley

Will I Be Famous?

Once upon a dream,
Oh, what's the theme?
Will I ever be famous, beautiful and rich?
Yeah, yeah, you're just going to buy a Nintendo Switch,
I could be a singer,
Or even a left-winger,
Just listen to my dreams,
I'd rather buy ice cream,
Come on, let me share my ambitions,
All my hard work and all my auditions,
What if I was a poet?
Then I really would know it!
The more we practise, the more we have hope,
We could be famous for sure,
But how would we cope?
Our dreams may come true,
Believe in me like I believe in you.

Grace Minton (8)
Oakley CE Junior School, Oakley

All Of My Dreams

Here is a poem,
About my dreams,
So let's go and explore them,
And I hope you adore them.

My first dream,
Is for the world to be made of food,
Where the clouds are cotton candy,
And nobody would be in a mood.

My next dream,
Is for school to start at 11 o'clock,
And to finish at three.
The teachers would get a shock.

My last dream is the best of them all,
Every Friday, everyone has to have pizza,
Followed by a movie night,
I hope you enjoyed it,
Because that is the end of all of my dreams.

Jessica Clacy (9)
Oakley CE Junior School, Oakley

Sweet Dreams

S weet little bees in the spring
W here in my dream are those bees?
E xiting little flowers
E nergetically flying through the air
T otally crazy but it's my dream

D reams are amazing, I really want to have one each night
R uthless nightmares get in the way
E nthusiastic birds flying through the air
A nd fantastic things
M agic dreams are the best
S o have a dream today.

Jack Meyer (9)
Oakley CE Junior School, Oakley

My Rock Dreams

Standing on stage, my heart was pounding like the fierce drums behind me.
The crowds were roaring like a roaring sea.
My foot started stamping as I began to play my first note and the words danced out of my mouth, making a beautiful tune.
I felt proud as the crowd started echoing my song back.
The lights were on me.
They were so bright like the diamond gems on my clothes.
This is it.
This is my dream.
This is my dream that will come true.

Heidi Day (7)
Oakley CE Junior School, Oakley

My Dreams

Last night, I had a dream I could soar higher than the stars
I saw birds below wistfully looking at my flying
I saw the treetops swaying in the breeze, tickling my toes
I saw swinging monkeys howling in the canopy
In Australia, I saw kangaroos trying to jump higher than me, but I still beat them
I saw wallabies trying to go faster, but right then, I was as fast as a racing car
"No one can beat me," I screamed.

Matilda Varian (9)
Oakley CE Junior School, Oakley

Potions

P *op, bang, boom!* Different coloured smoke comes
   out.

O h, the wizards are in funny cloaks.

T he pink smoke, blue smoke and the green.

I saw the dragons doing loop-the-loops.

O ne by one, I saw the fairies leave.

N ow it was dark and strange.

S piders came out, this only meant a new adventure
   was going to begin.

Carah Morris (8)
Oakley CE Junior School, Oakley

Dreams

Dreams can take you anywhere,
They can hypnotise you so that you stare.

Sometimes, dreams go way out of control,
You could be opera singing one minute,
Then the next, rock 'n' roll.

They can make you like an adult, all grown up
Or on a calm lake riding an SUP.

Dreams are my favourite mode of transportation
They can take you to a world of joy and imagination.

Aislinn Hughes (9)
Oakley CE Junior School, Oakley

Midnight

M y imagination will happen tonight
I nteresting dreams will happen all around the world
D reams are so special, so special
N o, no, to not a bad dream
I n my dream, I see monsters
G igantic monsters rush up to me
H elp someone
T he terrifying monsters go away, wait, I am awake.

Fatoumata Binta Bah (11)
Oakley CE Junior School, Oakley

Vets Care

V ets help animals so they can get better,
E very animal deserves love,
T hey come and I help,
S upporting, loving and caring.

C urly, straight, long or short hair,
A ll are included,
R eceiving healthcare,
E ven the wild or grumpy ones.

Leomi Lee-Buckland (8)
Oakley CE Junior School, Oakley

Sky Fly Axolotls

In my dreams every night,
Pink things fly with coloured light.
I look around. All I can see is smoke.
How did I get here? I hope it's not a joke!
One by one they pass me by,
They all fly off into the sky.
I notice they are axolotls, bright and fun,
Dancing happily around the sun.

Rio Chan (9)
Oakley CE Junior School, Oakley

Snake Waking Up To Breakfast

S nake wakes up and hisses to the sun
N ext, he goes and eats breakfast nicely
A t 7 o'clock at the zoo, he sheds
K ids go to see him and get excited
E nd of the day, Snake is fast asleep.

Lily Massey (8)
Oakley CE Junior School, Oakley

Dream Of Being A Vet

I dream of being a vet,
It has an X-ray,
It has a surgery room,
It has a table,
I really want to be a vet,
And I can't wait to be one too.

Holly Bennett (8)
Oakley CE Junior School, Oakley

The Beast

Every night I hear a sound,
It comes from deep under the ground,
When it crawls beneath my bed,
I feel a sudden urge of dread.
When it jumps out under me,
I never feel a jolt of glee.
It has a dark glistening red eye,
When I see it I want to die.
Its horns point up towards space,
It makes me run off at a pace.
Its black armour is shadowy and cold,
Even though it's centuries old.
It rides upon an evil hound,
When I see it, my heart starts to pound.
It has a massive spear,
When I see it I feel fear.
When the sunlight hits his knife,
He straight away turns to ice.

Elliott Ginn (9)
Queen Elizabeth's Hospital School, Clifton

The Royal Family

One day, I was walking around fast when I spotted a baby pony. It was in the middle of nowhere. I adopted it. I got it some clothes and then I had an idea, I was going to go to a whole new world but I did not know when to do it.

My pony grew, she was now fully grown. She knew what to do when I double-tapped her on her nose. It meant I was going on her back. When I tapped her once, it meant it was time to eat. When I stroked her, it was time to play.

I finally decided we were going to the forest on a path I had never been on. *I hope I don't get lost. Let's have a good night's rest.*

When I woke up, I didn't forget today was the day. I was going to leave and that's when a name popped into my head. My pony's name was Sprinkle, her name was perfect. I forgot about all my problems, I felt like I could only think about positive things. I double-tapped her nose. She slowly headed down and off we went. We passed a zillion flowers and then we arrived. I spotted a castle, there was a sign that said something. I couldn't read it, so I approached step by step until I could. The sign said: 'Look for the daughter'.

Before I went in, I tied Sprinkle with a rope and then I was inside the castle...

Ariane Amaral (8)
Sandbrook Community Primary School, Rochdale

The Dream I Dream Almost Every Night

The dream I dream almost every night,
Is the summer sun, so warm and bright.
It's on my skin, it's in my eyes,
With no clouds and pale blue skies.
We board the plane, we take our seat,
Another few hours till we're in the heat.
Jump in the pool, go down a slide,
Have a cold drink with ice cream on the side.
Climbing, exploring, seeing the sights,
Oh, I forgot, I'm afraid of heights.
Family time with lots of laughs,
I'd rather be here than doing maths.
Making memories to cherish forever,
Nothing beats time together.
As our time comes to an end,
Say goodbye to our newfound friends.
As I wake up in the morning,
With sleepy eyes and still yawning.
I brush my teeth and get ready for school,
Maths isn't too bad so that's cool.

Edie Warner (8)
Sandbrook Community Primary School, Rochdale

I Had A Dream, So Rare, So Real

I had a dream
At Sandbrook Park,
Children screaming
In the dark.

What was the reason
For this to happen?
A group of monsters
Who came from Saturn.

I had a dream, so rare, so real!

I had a dream
At Sandbrook Park,
Mr Taylor
Got eaten by a shark!

I tried to help
But it was too late,
I was scared myself
Which wasn't great!

I had a dream, so rare, so real!

I had a dream
At Sandbrook Park,
With monsters and animals
Like Noah's Ark.

Worried and scared
For my school,
I didn't expect this
It was supposed to be cool!

I had a dream, so rare, so real!

I woke up in the morning
My dream was no more,
Sumaiya was glad
That's me, for sure!

I had a dream, so rare, so real!

Sumaiya Wasim (9)
Sandbrook Community Primary School, Rochdale

A Monster In My Mind

Is there a monster living under my bed?
Or just a scary thought that I have in my head?
I've read about monsters at book club in school,
Of terrifying creatures and phantoms and ghouls,
Is the monster big or small?
Is that his shadow upon my wall?
Does he have teeth? Are his eyes big and round?
If he doesn't exist then what is that sound?
A creak and a bang,
My heart skips a beat,
Will the monster appear?
Is he looking to eat?
I pull up the covers,
Way up over my head,
I'm too scared to look,
Or get out of my bed,
But then I peep out,
I put on my brave hat,
And at the foot of my bed,
It's only my...
Cat!

Logan James Jones (8)
Sandbrook Community Primary School, Rochdale

The Beach

The sand, the shells, in between my toes.
The smell of fish and chips in my nose.
Sun, sun, in my eyes, the clouds so high in the sky.
Swim, swim, in the sea, "Oh no, there's a shark getting me!"

Riding donkeys on the sand, "Faster and faster," I demand.
Boats and planes are everywhere, in the sea and in the air.
Towels and beach balls everywhere, chilling out without a care.
Animals, animals, everywhere, in the distance you will see.
Sunglasses, sunglasses, on my eyes, it wasn't sunny till I arrived.
Come to the beach where the sea is bluer, and little white waves come running at you.

Esmae Boardman (8)
Sandbrook Community Primary School, Rochdale

Winter Unicorn

One winter,
A snow white unicorn,
Went for a walk,
She saw another,
Snow white unicorn,
We're twins, one thought,
But how? the other one thought,
It was like looking in a mirror,
She had a white body.
White, sparkly hair,
And baby blue eyes,
The unicorns went back to the village,
They told their parents,
Their parents said, "You are twins!"
Both unicorns were confused,
"What?" they both shouted,
"How?" they both shouted,
"You and me, twins? No, no, no."
"No way, you and me are twins? Just no way."

Olivia Speak (8)
Sandbrook Community Primary School, Rochdale

The Winter Fairy

The clumsy winter fairy sat on a tree
And flew up high
She saw a big winter dragon
That threw snowballs
The dragon had white scales

So she flew away
Until she saw another fairy
She thought it looked normal
But little did she know it was evil!

She went up to the fairy and said,
"Hi, I am Katie and you are?"
The other fairy said, "Hi, I am Jen."

But she noticed that Jen had glowing red eyes
The fairy flew fast and got far away
And went back home.

Michelle Okpara (8)
Sandbrook Community Primary School, Rochdale

Lightness And Darkness

Once in a universe, filled with light,
Where the sun shined super bright,
And everyone was their happiest selves,
But most of them looked like elves,
One day, disaster struck,
And everyone had bad luck,
Darkness took over light,
And the sun wasn't so bright,
The bright leaves turned dark,
And no one went to the park,
The universe became a darker place,
And everyone felt they had pie on their face,
We used to see a universe that was bright,
But sadly, darkness took over the light.

Chioma Peace (9)
Sandbrook Community Primary School, Rochdale

The Friendly Dragon

In a town, fear ran deep,
A dragon walked trying to bring peace to keep.
But the people trembled at his size,
Judging him with fear in their eyes.
Sitting alone, frowning and sad,
Until a brave girl made him glad.
"Don't be sad, everything will be fine,
I see the goodness in you, let your light shine."
With her help, the town soon saw,
That the dragon wasn't there to break their law.
So remember, don't judge by what you see,
For true kindness can set you free.

Hazel Lancaster (9)
Sandbrook Community Primary School, Rochdale

All About Me...

My name is Delphi, I am eight years old
I'm rather cute, so I'm told.

I love to dance and sing
But my favourite thing to do
Is play on a swing.

I like ice cream
I eat it day and night
Especially strawberry, it's a delight.

Blue is the best colour
It is the best colour of the skies
When the sun shines, it reflects my eyes.

I have a dog called Winnie
Her breed is a cockapoo
She acts like a human
And gives great kisses too.

Delphi Kershaw (8)
Sandbrook Community Primary School, Rochdale

Superpowers

S uperpowers are really cool, they can be

U sed for really good or bad,

P ower can be dangerous and can be found anywhere

E ven in the sand

R eal people can be saved from tough times

P owers are sometimes as bad as crimes

O thers can let the power get to their heads

W e must make sure we put it in the right hands

E ventually we will make the world a better place

R eally try to make sure everyone is

S afe.

Excellent Ukpebor (9)
Sandbrook Community Primary School, Rochdale

The Twinkling Stars

The shiny yellow stars
The bright white moon
Hope I see you soon!
The very next day
I am on my way
To school obviously
"Hi, I'm Lily."
It is my first day
I'm scared okay
The shiny bright moon
Twinkling stars too
I miss them all
I'm really tall
So I can see all
Big and small
Finally, once more
I feel so sore
From the work I did
I'll set myself on mild
Hey, but at least I see it again...

Habibah Mobeen (8)
Sandbrook Community Primary School, Rochdale

Sweet Dreams

I climb and climb the stairs to rest my sleepy head.
I close my eyes as I drift and drift away to a land called
Candy Bay.
I lick and lick my lips from the taste of sour green,
green grass.
I bounce and bounce along the clouds of beautiful
candyfloss.
I swoop and swoop through the sky, upon my unicorn's
back.
I dream and dream away of a poodle, pink and blue.
I see and see all the beautiful trees and the flowers
too.
I really wish and wish my dream would come true.

Matilda Ida Pedley (9)
Sandbrook Community Primary School, Rochdale

Magical World!

I take a step onto a train,
I look out of the window at the drops of rain.
I end up at Hogwarts in the Forbidden Forest,
Feeling out of place, feeling like a tourist.
Potions and spells, Hogwarts has it all,
Books and brooms, high castle walls.
Wands, magical creatures, these are just a few,
In the great hall, you can name them too!
In the game of Quidditch you rise and fall,
Whatever you can think of, Hogwarts has it all.

Aniya Ariana Habib (8)

Sandbrook Community Primary School, Rochdale

Superpowers

S uperpowers are so cool,
U seful like a good tool.
P eople are saved,
E very hero is brave.
R unning to help people,
P ersuading villains to be equal.
O verall powers are positive,
W hen they could also be negative.
E veryone might not deserve powers,
R uining famous towers.
S uperpowers, does everyone deserve them?

Marwa Imran (9)
Sandbrook Community Primary School, Rochdale

Unique Unicorn!

A unique unicorn,
Got warned!
She was so shocked,
She walked away!
Then she stopped and knocked,
Her mother responded!
She was so tired,
So the unique unicorn,
Trudged to her bed!

Haniya Aslam Rasheed (9)
Sandbrook Community Primary School, Rochdale

The Forgotten Dream

In my galaxy, anything is possible.
Mythical creatures roam in my dome.
Cotton candy clouds watch everything from above.
In the caves below, sea dragons go.
In a pond or stream, they like to dream.
In the sky or clouds, wind dragons jump about.
In the air, with no care.
In space, galaxy dragons sing, no sadness here,
everyone is vibing.
Deep in a forest,
somebody has arrived.
Who are these creatures?
Maybe they've come to thrive,
so I go and start greeting.
But because of what I see, I end up eating
my nails, sharper than a knife,
became blunter than lead.
"Humans?"
My head became heavy.
"What are they doing here?"
"Oh no, are they here for the rainbow orb?"

Sreevidya Veeravalli (10)
St Anne's Catholic Primary School, Weeping Cross

The Mysterious Adventure

It was time to go to bed,
And to rest my sleepy head.
I climbed the stairs up to my room,
Then I looked out the window and saw the glistening moon.
I tried hard to get to sleep,
So, I counted some cosy sheep.
Finally, I jumped into the world of dreams,
And I wondered what it all meant.
A girl stood looking there for miles,
And all she could see were trees with smiles.
The trees sat, a gleam between the gaps,
And suddenly, some twigs went *snap!*
She walked off further to look for more,
Her legs got so tired and sore.
All of a sudden, she heard a *splish splash!*
So her slow walk turned into a dash!
She ran quickly and pushed the leaves out of her face,
And she felt like she had joined a race.
The further and further she gets,
The more the ground got soaking wet.
Finally, she came to a stop,
And her mouth dropped open in shock.

In front of her was a mighty waterfall,
The scenery was like a grand hall.
The sounds it made, were a *splish splash*,
And the more it did, the more it made the girl's mouth drop.
The dream said goodbye and disappeared,
But you never know if it will come back next year.

Eva McGarrigle (10)
St Anne's Catholic Primary School, Weeping Cross

Over The Moon!

I can feel joy entering my body,
I'm the first female to do it,
I can just glimpse my family and friends,
Frantically offering their hands for me,
Clapping their hands at the sight of the first woman
On the moon.
Me!
I adored it,
The blood pumping through my veins,
At the feeling of being here,
I didn't care about the thin, foggy air,
Or the lack of oxygen,
So I took a step...

My foot didn't touch the ground again,
I was defying gravity,
And no one,
Was going to bring me down,
I lifted my other foot,
I was off the ground, soaring!
I didn't want it to stop,
Ever!
I didn't want to set foot

In that rocket again,
I didn't want to set foot
On Earth again,
For I was delighted here,
More delighted than I'd ever been,
Ever!

Pippa Hegarty (10)
St Anne's Catholic Primary School, Weeping Cross

Luxury Life

Bing, bang, bong!
Loud footsteps coming here,
Louder and louder,
It's very near.
All of my family and friends come to stay,
For a very fun long day.

Luxury items here and there,
If you can see it everywhere,
Relaxing and having fun,
Just wait there,
The party's not done.

Running around on the stairs,
Playing games like truth or dare,
Swimming in the pool,
With friends looking cool.

The clear water spinning everywhere,
People going anywhere,
Friends and family running around,
Loud cheers, can you hear the sound?

On a long table with a variety of food,
People smile with a positive mood,
Kids are now very full,
Tug of war, their rope is getting pulled.

The party is now over,
Wait till next time it's a sleepover.

Michelle Adedugbe (10)
St Anne's Catholic Primary School, Weeping Cross

My Pure Imagination

I closed my eyes and fell asleep,
I thought, *where am I going tonight?*
I was strumming my guitar,
But it was quite bizarre,
There were musical, magical notes forming a fairy,
She was called Mary.
My house turned into a palace,
My rug started to fly,
On my bed were some potions,
I grabbed them and... *Whoosh!*
My guitar started to cry,
We landed on a cloud made out of cotton candy.
That's what I could see,
It was as sweet as can be,
I went everywhere,
One place was the house of the mayor.
It was my imagination, taking me wherever I thought,
I went to the beach,
Visited the moon,
Then landed in a giant peach.
I accidentally landed in a bee hive.
Then I had a knife,
A cow kicked me out,

Ouch!
I had a pout,
And woke up on the couch.

Orla Byrne (9)
St Anne's Catholic Primary School, Weeping Cross

Space Cat

Cats rule the world here,
Cats here and there,
If you stick out,
Or if you feel tired,
And if you feel wired,
You can fly away to the moon,
Zoom!

Your worries are gone,
As you see a flying cat,
Friendly and fat,
In the starry sky,
Dancing around.

"*Meow*," says the cat,
Sweet, round and fat,
As he eats a packet of crisps.

You turn around,
And you are taken by surprise,
As all you see is gingerbread,
Gingerbread houses,
Gingerbread sculptures,

Gingerbread everything
And more.

The time has come
For you to leave this place behind.
So you say goodbye,
And hitch a ride,
Back to your bed again.

You wake up with a yawn,
And it is down,
As you see,
That it was all just a dream.

Rebecca Ashby (9)
St Anne's Catholic Primary School, Weeping Cross

Out Of This World

I wake up in an unusual place,
To find that I'm in outer space!
I open my eyes,
And find starry skies,
That are as beautiful as light!

Two goals cross over my eyes,
My heart begins to rise.
The ball in the centre,
My friends are getting ready,
I run, without being steady,
I kick the ball,
As hard as a mall,
It zooms towards the net,
Looking impossible to get,
Bang!
It flies through the back of the net!

My friends look around,
To find bits of the net on the ground,
And the goal sets alight.
As if it were saying goodnight!

Down and down I go,
About to say no...
But I just fall asleep again.

Luke Harland (10)
St Anne's Catholic Primary School, Weeping Cross

My Minecraft Dream

I spawned into a world.
Everything was blocky.
I realised it was Minecraft.
I went to a tree.
It broke in a few punches.
I was amused.
I broke more because it was satisfying.
Green grass littered the landscape.
I crafted oak planks and one crafting table.
With a few sticks that I got, I made a pickaxe.
I saw a cave nearby.
I was stunned by how deep it was.
I got down by a stream and found stone.
I mined the hard stone and got a stone pickaxe.
I built a base.
When the sun was rising, I found diamonds.
It was hard, but I got obsidian to make a portal.
When I lit the portal, I went in.

Stephan Basson (10)
St Anne's Catholic Primary School, Weeping Cross

I Am A Cat

I'm a cat in the savannah,
With an owner called Hannah.
We live in a house of wood and stone,
It suits us so well, we call it home.

However one day I did spot,
A pride of lions in a pot,
Then a wizard appeared,
His face was submerged in a hairy beard.
He was to make a potion!
I was filled with emotion.

I ran over to help,
But jumped back with a yelp!
The wizard and lions were gone,
Only the sun, from a cloud, now shone.
Had I imagined it?
No way could they fit.
So I ran back home,
To the house of wood and stone.

Ailen Colville (10)
St Anne's Catholic Primary School, Weeping Cross

Once Upon A Dream

Me and my friend
Come to explore
But not anymore
We get lost
In the woods
With no one around
Not even a sound
Then we spot
With a single eye
A house.
We walk over
And find
What I love
A house
With chocolate
With drizzles of toffee
Sauce.
A blob of
Ice cream!
But a little more
With sprinkles and
Cotton candy galore!

This house is like
My dream house.
But next door
To this house
Is a whole chocolate river
With a chocolate waterfall
The chocolate
River slowly drizzles
Down the hill
With yummy doughnuts
Around the bottom.

Evelyn Markland (10)
St Anne's Catholic Primary School, Weeping Cross

Dreams

Dreams are mysterious blessings
Some can bring everything you've ever wanted to life
Others can pull your worst fears from the darkness
And bring them to life
But here is my dream
I'm in a different dimension
Straight from my imagination
I'm paralysed between a brutal battle
Suddenly, before my eyes
My feet are leaving the floor
I'm starting to fly!
But my joy starts to fade,
As everything around me turns into horrible
Spiders!
But right when I think it's over for me,
I wake up in bed, as safe as can be.

Arthur Ferraz (10)
St Anne's Catholic Primary School, Weeping Cross

Pokémon Land

The sun yawns as it rises for the cold morning
It is weird in Pokémon Land
It has trees as pixelated as Minecraft
And a sky as clear as can be
The wind whooshes as the sun smiles
Out onto the world of Pokémon Land
Next to my leg sits lightning-yellow Pikachu
Pokémon, big and small,
Crawl all over the depths of the dark, scary forest
The grass dances in the whoosh of the wind
Pokémon greet you as you enter these lands
But make sure you are alert
For you never know when they might hurt.

Max Dillon (10)
St Anne's Catholic Primary School, Weeping Cross

Llama Land!

I am teleported to a funny-looking place,
But I feel that I'm in outer space!
Surrounded by llamas, I stare in awe,
How have I never been here before?

Some llamas, creamy, some llamas, brown,
I can't see a worry, not even a frown!
I climb on a llama, puffy and soft,
A few heavy steps and *whoosh!* we're off.

My heart thumps in wonder, this land is so cool!
But what if someone is pranking me, am I a fool?
I close my eyes, not a hint of dread,
I open again, and I'm back in my bed!

Sofia Salt (10)
St Anne's Catholic Primary School, Weeping Cross

Planets

I am on Earth, so I went to the moon.
I met an alien friend called Moo.
We became friends and played too.

On Jupiter, I found a friend,
You will never know who.
His name was Dupler.
Sadly I have to say bye,
To my other friend Moo.

On Saturn looking at the rings,
We stood there with Dupler,
And Moo came to see.
Hoping that the stars will shine and gleam.
Like the sunset meets the sea.

Going back home,
To the green and blue.
Land and ocean.
Where boats sail,
And houses are made.

Olivia Giannaki (10)
St Anne's Catholic Primary School, Weeping Cross

The Void

As you lie in your bed
You are as sweaty as a thread
The windows flood pitch-black
The house becomes silent
Until the walls fade away like dust
The black emptiness surrounds you
You drift through time
And it's not fine
The barrier breaks open
And the void starts to open
And you get taken
The grey stone stands from
More industrial builds, it looks like
The white fog all around speaks from behind
And the mysteries that lie beneath
The only thing you have is your *mind.*

Jake Witkowski (10)
St Anne's Catholic Primary School, Weeping Cross

Colourful Fish

In my dreams every night,
I can't get it off my mind,
Me and my friends were walking by,
When something caught our eye,
A massive sign high above,
Saying swim with colourful fish,
I started convincing them to come in,
Until they gave in,
We stepped in and you won't believe,
All the colourful fish staring at me,
I got excited and jumped in,
An hour passed by and I didn't want to leave,
Until I saw an ice cream van across from me.

Sophia Lloyd (10)
St Anne's Catholic Primary School, Weeping Cross

Once Upon A Dream

I lie down and close my eyes in bed,
Where am I now?
I think,
Fairies and unicorns are all I see,
And delicious houses as sweet as can be.
Pink birds are flying everywhere,
And purple trees are dancing in the air,
I hear somebody call my name:
"Come on,
Come on,
I'm over here!"
It wakes me up,
Oh no,
Oh dear!
Just then I wake up,
Then I realise it's just my sister screaming in my ear.

Freddie Wallbank (9)
St Anne's Catholic Primary School, Weeping Cross

Dreams In Space

Space, it is a mysterious place.
The stars shine like metal.
The planets dance with joy.
The sun shines like gold.

The Milky Way waves at the planets.
The magical animals whoosh across the sky.
Neil Armstrong and I want to go and fly.
I told a lie
So I could go and fly, wheee!

It is time to say goodbye.
My time is up.
The planets and stars wave goodbye.
My imagination can fly.
I will see you next time.

Raife Sims (9)
St Anne's Catholic Primary School, Weeping Cross

Flying Penguins

Nothing has prepared me for this amazing land I see,
I take a step forward,
As astonished as can be,
Sophia and me side by side,
In the crystal clear sky,
As we wait for flying penguins to pass by,
They give us a high five,
We are still shocked that we are alive,
I am as excited as can be,
And Sophia is just as elated as me,
Suddenly, there was a flash of light,
I jumped and I realised it was just the night.

Zuzanna Rzaczkiewicz (10)
St Anne's Catholic Primary School, Weeping Cross

My Beautiful Family In The City

In the galaxy-looking sky
In the city
All my friends and family came
We all went to a beautiful garden
The sun shone on the colourful flowers
But suddenly, it rained
My family was in such pain
It started happy and joyful
But now it's sad and painful
Happily, the rain stopped
We talked and walked all the way home
The next day, we went to a beach
The same thing happened again.

Angelin Juby (10)
St Anne's Catholic Primary School, Weeping Cross

My Magical Dream World

It is upside down in Dream World,
Flying blackbirds below your feet,
Glowing sun in the morning sky,
Fluffy velvet clouds on your feet,
Happy time jumping on clouds,
The sky is as green as a forest,
The dangling trees dance in the elegant wind.
The birds sing wonderful songs.
It is a peaceful place,
When it is right,
You are gazing at the stars,
Dozing in your bed.

Emilia Fletcher (9)
St Anne's Catholic Primary School, Weeping Cross

Flying

I was once looking up at the sky,
Then all of a sudden, goodbye!
I zoomed off my seat,
And clouds were dancing past my feet!
The sky was a beautiful blue,
And I was saying to myself,
"Is this really true?
Oh please, make it be,
This is the best place in the whole galaxy!"
I was flying high!
Why?
I don't know.
I just didn't want to go!

Ava Woolley (9)
St Anne's Catholic Primary School, Weeping Cross

A Dream

There are talking animals,
They are as noisy as a chatterbox,
The ground is yellow,
And the sky is purple,
The animals sing a song,
As the people talk so long,

The animals escape,
While the people have a debate,
Babies crawl around,
As people jump up and down,
The birds fly so high,
As parents always lie.

Ethika Sangeeth (10)
St Anne's Catholic Primary School, Weeping Cross

Wielding The Power

The world in front of me,
Crashing waves on the sea,
Me and my friends laugh with glee,
"Time for fun," we say.
We shape the world like it's made of clay.
One of us creates lots of volts,
Zap! Zap! We throw lightning bolts.
We create rainfall as clear as glass,
The fun we had had to pass.

Leo Fearns (10)
St Anne's Catholic Primary School, Weeping Cross

Light To Dark

Light to dark, left grass all around me.
Birds humming, animals running.
Fog and mist come though.
Darkness follows me.
Animals disappear into the foggy mist.
Darkness finally *whooshed* away.
Only me and little lamb left.
Baby tiger carefully walks through.
Only me, a little tiger and lamb left.

Nicole Kayibabu (10)
St Anne's Catholic Primary School, Weeping Cross

The Crystal Sky

I woke up in a place,
Where I could go anywhere in the world,
Planes flew through the crystal blue sky,
And white figures appeared.
But I took them out and saw all of the world,
It looked like it was a red crystal but on fire.

Yuvraj Singh Tiwana (10)
St Anne's Catholic Primary School, Weeping Cross

My Dream

I'm flying on my dragon,
Her name is Violet,
We're going to Crazy Land,
You can do anything there,
You can play in your imagination,
Whoosh!
You've got superpowers,
Your imagination!

Sophie Thomas (10)
St Anne's Catholic Primary School, Weeping Cross

Black Hole

A black void appears from a massive black hole
There are a lot of planets
Some have life
Some are like our Solar System
Some are stars
There's no end in there
Will I ever come out from there?

Jazz Ling (10)
St Anne's Catholic Primary School, Weeping Cross

Penguin

P enguin Land is cold,

E xtraordinarily bold,

N ever hot nor warm,

G laciers are being torn,

U nder the sea,

I ce is above me,

N o one ever leaves here.

Sophia Thompson-Attwooll (10)
St Anne's Catholic Primary School, Weeping Cross

Dream

D reaming of a pirate ship or fairies in the sky, one thing that I know is it's a dream in the night,

R hinos with magic hats full of cats with bats, a dream can be anything!

E legant ballerinas dancing at a show, then in comes a lion to end it with a roar,

A mazing acrobatics flipping in the sky,

M onsters chasing you, he catches up and ends it with a bite, you wake up startled and say, "What a night!"

Zack Howard (11)
Stakesby Primary Academey, Whitby

The Transporting Treasure Chest

I open my eyes to this strange world I see.
Suddenly, Layla, my best friend,
Appears right next to me.
We look around the dirty place,
And see a very scary face.

Smoke rises above my head,
Then I look up with dread.
The beastly eyes glow and come towards us,
A monster crawls, but we look left and right.
And then we turn on the torch and see two wings,
The creature must be a dragon.
The firelit sky turns shades of red,
A golden glint in the distance!

Suddenly, Mila appears,
We look around and then the dragon disappears.
The golden spark is seen again,
What could it be?

We walk around the dusty place and see a volcano,
We hear a *boom!* Uh-oh!
We need to hurry before it erupts.

Then we see lava,
Flowing down the steep rocky hill.
As soon as it touches the ground,
The island turns as bright as can be!
We are saved!

The golden glint appears once again,
As we follow the sparkle,
We see a wizard turning an apple tree nice and green.

We find the treasure chest and *poof!*
I'm back in bed!

Elise Townshend (8)
Stakesby Primary Academey, Whitby

A Dark Monster

A dark monster,
A terrifying thing.
I see it in my garden,
My family is disappearing...
I do not know what to do,
At night it follows me.
It hides on the top of buildings.
I see it killing people. It's getting too far.
It's quiet — it's here.
The lights are out, I can't see.
There's light... I'm scared.
Aah!
It's just a nightmare.

Riley Leeman (8)
Stakesby Primary Academey, Whitby

The Girl Who Fell Into A Well

Once upon a time, on an abandoned island full of ghosts, a girl called Fern got stuck on the island. All of the ghosts pushed her into a well and she called for help.

Her big sister, Mia, tried to help her, but the ghosts pushed her in too. They were shouting really loudly and their friend Emilie helped them. They lived happily ever after.

Emilie Newton (8)
Stakesby Primary Academey, Whitby

Dinosaurs With Superpowers

Last night my dinosaurs came to life,
We travelled back in time,
It was a wonderful sight.

Tyrannosaurus, with strength untold,
Could shake the ground and make mountains fold.
Its roaring voice could split the skies,
With a power that made all creatures realise.

Triceratops, with horns aglow,
Could bring wild storms and make winds blow.
Its ancient wisdom, deep and grand,
Could shake the world and the land.

Stegosaurus, with armoured back,
Could turn invisible in a flash attack.
Its spiky tail, a weapon so true,
Could pierce through any foe, no clue.

Velociraptors, with speed so swift,
Could teleport in a mystical rift.
Their cunning minds, a force to fear,
Could outsmart any enemy near.

Pterodactyls, with wings spread wide,
Could control the oceans and the tide.
Their majestic flight, a sight so grand,
Could soar above the skies, a magical land.

So in my dinosaur dream set a long time ago,
Their superpowers put on a spectacular show.
When I woke up they weren't sitting in a row,
Did this really happen? Where did they go?

Layton Ferguson (10)
Valley Primary School, Whitehaven

The Crazy Rainbow Of Secrets

In a rainbow world sat a rainbow school,
There was a colour that wasn't red, green or blue,
She looked nice, she looked cool,
But she had a secret that made her feel like a fool,
People bullied her, especially the Queens of Green,
Who were a group of mean teens,
But she was used to it, if you woke up in her dream,
She'd still have a bad day anyway, it seemed,
She just wished she could float up in the air,
Doing weird dances without any care,
Taking her wig off and swinging her hair,
That was her secret - she was bald,
Her parents thought it wasn't fair,
Neither did her brother,
But that's because he wanted it to wear,
But if she told her bullies,
They'd probably stick a needle in her eyeball as a dare,
Lying in her room with the lights off,
Wondering if her bullies had a fear,
Maybe a dwarf calf or the height of a giraffe,
She'll think for a while,
Till she finds out and returns her smile.

In a rainbow world sat a rainbow school,
Entered a colour that was now blue.

Bella Rose Plaskett (9)
Valley Primary School, Whitehaven

Savage Space Spiders

As the sun says goodbye,
And the moon emerges in the sky,
Some peculiar creatures come to swing by.

As the stars peer down,
And the cars drive around,
Some colossal arachnids
Stumble through the alleyway grounds.

They have a lot of eyes,
So don't try to attack them,
Or you'll meet their demise.

A lot of people fear them,
They can cause a lot of mayhem,
They make a fair amount of trouble,
But way too much rubble,
But they came to our planet,
Whilst bringing an intense amount of racket.

With a *crash*, a *boom*, a *pow!*
They wander right through the town,
But they're trying to find one thing,
Their smart but missing king.

As I wake up from my dream,
My eyes emit a gleam,
The moon has said goodbye,
The sun emerges in the sky.

Dunamis Obong (10)
Valley Primary School, Whitehaven

Man Vs World

This man tried everything but one thing, he couldn't get a job.

His name was Bob without a job.

He went to the pub and got a pint, after that he was drunk, so he got a Sprite.

But one day, there was a portal with a turtle, that introduced him.

He said, "In this portal, anything comes true."

He thought, *can I get a job?*

He then opened his gob, "Will I be Bob with a job?"

They had some banter and got some Fanta.

He drifted through the air, making holes in the delicious clouds.

Then he decided to become a unicorn trainer, with sculptures made of candyfloss.

He tossed a coin.

If it landed on 'tails', he would get the job.

If it landed on 'heads', he wouldn't.

It landed on 'tails'. Would Bob get the job?

It arrived in the post. It said approved.

His name is Bob with a job.

Teddy Lynch (9)
Valley Primary School, Whitehaven

Spikes And Tails

In a world of fantasy and more,
There lived a dragon,
He was quite small.
He lived where volcanoes surrounded him,
And mountains towered over.

One day, a dragon named Spike,
Went out for a hike,
But that day gave him a shock!
Did I tell you this dragon couldn't fly?
This one day, he flew really high.

This day was a horrendous storm,
But he didn't know that it wasn't the norm.
This day the wind waved, the lightning struck,
But it was too strong...

He flew with the wind raising him up,
He flew within the sky,
He opened his eyes,
Was it all a dream?
I mean, I don't know,
It's not what it seems...

Mabel Goode (9)
Valley Primary School, Whitehaven

The Walking T-Shirt

A T-shirt is a T-shirt,
Nothing special at all,
Except for Ava McGregor's,
Whose T-shirt was called Paul.

Paul was full of mischief,
Naughty, rude and dumb,
When she tried to hang him out one day,
He slapped her on the bum!

He ran off to the fish shop,
To buy himself some chips,
Then sneaked off to the harbour,
To sit and watch the ships.

Ava tried to catch him,
But no matter how hard she tried,
He was always so much faster,
And could find great places to hide.

But sometimes life is cruel,
It's not all fun and games,
Ava was bored with his naughtiness,
So bought a new T-shirt called James.

Millie Hanlon-Nixon (9)
Valley Primary School, Whitehaven

Dreamland

At night when I close my eyes,
And dream of magical places,
My imagination takes me on a journey,
To stars, seas and other extraordinary spaces.

Where the grass is pink,
And the skies are green,
Mountains are topped
With vanilla ice cream.
Lollipop trees,
And candyfloss clouds,
And eye-catching birds,
That sing very loud.
Where rivers are made
Out of chocolate,
Milk, dark and white,
And you hold your breath softly,
As you take in the sight.

At night, when I close my eyes,
And I dream of magical places,
My imagination takes me on a journey,
To stars, seas and other extraordinary spaces.

Eva Hanlon-Nixon (9)
Valley Primary School, Whitehaven

World Cup Dream

I dream I can see a football pitch with Ronaldo and his teammates. The other team is right next to him, springing onto the football pitch, ready to play against Argentina.

Portugal is trying to win the World Cup. I hope he wins, if he loses I will probably be heartbroken... and so will he.

Portugal is winning 1-0. Yes! He scored a penalty! Now it is 2-0. Oh no, it's 2-1. Argentina nearly scored a goal! Yeah! It's 3-1. Portugal have won! Ronaldo is number one. Ronaldo, Ronaldo, Ronaldo! Yes! He is the best ever player. Portugal starts to celebrate after winning the World Cup. Colourful confetti floats in the air, as they hold the cup in the sky.

Lily Meldrum (9)
Valley Primary School, Whitehaven

The Upside-Down World

In the upside-down world,
Everything is flipped,
Nothing is natural,
I did believe it,
I just wasn't expecting this!

Flowers bloom in the sky,
The upside-down world is wonderful,
I wonder why?

The birds fly at my feet,
I never want to leave.
Trees are brushing my hair,
Floating around without a care.

The sky is green,
The ground is blue,
The upside-down world is new,
And still, we have no clue.

Me and Layla (that's my dog),
We love to explore, but that's not enough,
We heard a scream then we woke up,
Nobody knows what it was!

Ada McGregor (9)
Valley Primary School, Whitehaven

The Hungry Underpants

These underpants love their food,
If you talk to them, they'll give you attitude.
They're very good with their laser eyes,
Don't leave any food about, especially pies.

Underpants hate their food cold,
Like an ageing man when he's getting old,
The underpants' belly roars like a burning devil,
Their anger goes to a whole different level.

These underpants are very special,
No one can hurt them, they're made of metal,
It's very rare to see them happy,
I think their new name should be *Snappy.*

Rory Hodgkiss (10)
Valley Primary School, Whitehaven

Pirates And Fairies

Pirates came to my window,
And they put me in a sack closed tight,
They gave me rope to fiddle with
And they took me to their land.

The pirates gave me an important job,
To spy on the fairies,
The fairies were at the lagoon,
They took the pirates' treasure.

I went to the lagoon,
The fairies were there,
They were flying next to it,
They caught me trying to steal the treasure.

I was in trouble,
The fairies flew over to me,
The pirates were mad,
What had I done?

Eve Wilkinson (9)
Valley Primary School, Whitehaven

Captain Wonderpants

When the city gets bare,
Captain Wonderpants is there.

When the city gets blown up,
Captain Wonderpants shows up.

When the city gets attacked,
Captain Wonderpants never cracks.

When the city gets swept up,
Captain Wonderpants brings the Incredible Hulk.

When the city is in trouble,
Captain Wonderpants is the double.

When the city comes to an end,
Captain Wonderpants can try to fend.

When the city cheers,
Captain Wonderpants has no fears.

Oliver Bradshaw (10)
Valley Primary School, Whitehaven

Nightwing

N ow I see a dragon roaming my street,

I t comes out at night, the wings blend with the stars.

G liding into the midnight sky, hiding from daytime,

H e hoops around the moon and follows the cars,

T ime after time, he ends up in my garden.

W hen he leaves, I leave some meat out for him.

I close my eyes, wondering if he ate it,

N ames flowed through my mind, then it came to me.

G reathunter was the perfect name! I hope to see him again soon...

Felicity Rose Pearson (10)
Valley Primary School, Whitehaven

The Magic Secret

M agical, mystical, mysterious,
A fter dinner, we went to explore,
G lazing fire danced down the hall,
I n the castle we heard a call, coming from a secret door,
C oming closer, Lola barked,

S lowly, carefully, cautiously, I opened the door,
E yeing the object, it was a necklace,
C ursing me to come closer,
R egretting going further... I ran,
E rasing the memory of the dream,
T ime's up! Thank goodness it is over.

Willow Hazelwood (10)
Valley Primary School, Whitehaven

The Space Snakes

As I fell asleep, I began to dream,
About two space snakes that fell in a race,
I tried to help but I stayed away,
The snakes looked like they were going to cry,
So I helped them fly as I said goodbye,
They were quite shy so it didn't work.

I tried and tried, so I came up with a new
Idea, even though I had a fever,
I will build them their own planet!
So I got some bricks,
Along with some sticks,
And built it and they lived in it.

Tyler Cardy (9)
Valley Primary School, Whitehaven

Monsters Everywhere

The monsters, they are everywhere,
In the closet, under the bed,
And in the dark alleyway.
Hiding in the shadows,
They have no mercy.
They are afraid of light,
So keep the lights on
And have a fright.

Once midnight strikes,
Prepare for the worst,
At this haunted time,
They emerge from the darkness.
When they arrive,
It's fight or flight,
Those white, glowing eyes,
Glaring back at you,
Oh, what a fright!

Evren Ozdemir (9)
Valley Primary School, Whitehaven

The Hungry Hoover

Last night I saw a Hoover acting funny,
A man went to grab some honey,
It was funny.
The next day, it got up and started running on the street,
He was in a race and got beat.
After that, he went to the chip shop to get some chips,
When he got the chips he got a side of dips.
The man came home to the smell of chips,
He went to the room and saw the hungry Hoover eating,
He decided to get rid of the hungry Hoover,
The house was finally quiet.

Carlton Ennis (9)
Valley Primary School, Whitehaven

Superpowers

I soar through the streets with my super speed,
As I run away from dangerous threats,
I zoom through danger to safety,
But no one answers me,
No one can see me!
I gave a fright but left at sight,
More bad guys came, no time to waste,
Mech Destroyer is coming to save the day with my
super speed.

Daven Mason (10)
Valley Primary School, Whitehaven

Rise Of The Red And Whites

Once upon a time, there was a boy,
His dream was to play football.
He wanted to be like Wayne Rooney.
He could run on a football pitch like he could run a
marathon.
He could kick a ball as fast as a rocket.
If you have a dream to chase, go as fast as a Blitzen
Jet.
One night, the moon shone on the football pitch,
His heart shone and reached out to every spectator
there at Wembley.
He wanted to be the one that scored goals and
performed well.
But to show people he really could, he had to work
hard at school.
Then he would do well at football.
But most of all, you have to rock up at football training,
have the right standard attitude.
Most importantly, at school you have to do the same
for everything.

Jackson Ward (9)
Yohden Primary School, Peterlee

Candy Wonderland

C otton candy dissolves on my tongue,
A nimals made of candy race around the land.
N erds flying through the clouds like birds,
D elicious candy piled up in towers,
Y ou couldn't imagine anything better,

W ander around as much as you can,
O h no, sugar rush!
N aughty Tic Tacs sprinting away,
D ummy lollies,
E nvy and Layla couldn't stop laughing,
R olling down the gummy bear hill,
L ollipop trees glisten in the sunlight,
A re you loving this dream?
N utella flows down the chocolate hill
D o you want to return to this dream?

Envy Devine
Yohden Primary School, Peterlee

Candy Wonderland

C otton candy just melted in my mouth.

A nimals of candy were running around.

N erds flying around like birds.

D elicious pancakes with more stuff.

Y ou can eat as much as you want.

W ander around as much as you want.

O h no – sugar rush!

N aughty Tic Tacs ran away.

D ummy lollies hanging from trees.

E nvy and Layla were running about.

R acing down the hill, they fell into a cotton candy bush.

L ayla and Envy couldn't stop laughing.

A re you having fun?

N utella river is over there!

D eep in the chocolate river.

Layla Robinson (9)
Yohden Primary School, Peterlee

Nightmare

N othing has prepared me for this strange land, I see,

I take a step forward, as nervous as can be,

G lancing left and right, all I see is smoke,

H elp! I don't like this terrible dream, get me out,

T angled in the vines, I am trapped, I want to escape back to my dream,

M ore smoke appears and fills my lungs, so I can't breathe,

A nt crawling over my body, itching my skin all over,

R eady to escape, I scream, roaring as loud as a lion,

E xcept no noise comes out, no one can hear me, I am terrified of this nightmare.

Maya Hardy (9)
Yohden Primary School, Peterlee

Fairytale Land

F rom a distance, it looks like

A magical land with unicorns

I n the castle. The prince's

R oyal party was starting

Y ou can see the fireworks setting off, and it looks magical

T ale in fairyland

A ngrily, the monster appeared

L ifting off the ground, flapping its wings

E bony sighed, "Is this a dream?"

L aughing, the monster was fine

A dancer was screaming

N ow in happiness, they

D anced happily ever after.

Ava Tanney (8)
Yohden Primary School, Peterlee

Football Player

Always believe because one day ago,
I woke up and I was playing as Vinicius Jr.
Then, like two minutes later,
I was in the locker room with Ancelotti the manager.
Then I was greeted by the janitor
And Bellingham came over,
Flying at the Atletico Madrid personal trainer.
We went up against Barcelona and won 2-1.
It was the Champions League final,
It was 2-2 and it went to penalties.
3-3 - what will happen?
I had everything on my back,
And I scored and we won it!
Best dream ever.

Luka Lonsdale (9)
Yohden Primary School, Peterlee

The Helping Tree

H arry was a boy who lived alone
E very day, he would talk to the helping tree
L ong ago, he planted it
P lanning that one day it would be amazing
I n the afternoon, he would visit
N ight was his favourite time to go
G limmering stars shone brightly

"T rees are amazing!" he would say
R on would sometimes come
E motions are held in the tree
E veryone loves it.

Ariyah Thomson (9)
Yohden Primary School, Peterlee

A World Of My Own

Imagination

I n my own imagination
M y dreams come true
A m I the only one who dreams?
G liding through the clouds
I am an awesome acrobat
N o one can bend or be more flexible than me!
A re you a dreamer, too?
T umbling and twisting, I make strange shapes.
I magine being me,
O h, what fun it would be,
N ow I am off to dream!

Esmae Nixon
Yohden Primary School, Peterlee

Football

F or tonight, I close my eyes

O h, how may I dream of the sunshine?

O f the day I dreamed it came to me, the game of football is all I need.

T hen the crowd screamed, "Yes!"

B all, the ball is in the goal

A ll the crowd cheered for me because I scored a goal for my team,

L oud and clear, I hear the fear

L ike the dinosaurs are near.

Layton Prince (9)
Yohden Primary School, Peterlee

Castle

My castle is like a beautiful queen looking over her
land,
Surrounded by the golden sand.
The castle is made of gold,
The knight stands tall and bold.
In Norway, the mountains are covered in snow.
They are pointed and grand,
I hope my wealth expands.
All you can hear is a marching band,
Unplanned, the queen went to sleep against the king's
demands.

Freddie Anderson (9)
Yohden Primary School, Peterlee

Candyland

C andy is delicious in Candyland
A re you done with your chores? So, get candy from Candyland
N ame your kind of candy to get it
D o you love candy?
Y ou think, *candy, yum,* then eat
L ove candy
A re you sure you love candy?
N ow, let's eat some candy
D o you think I love candy?

Isabella Peters (9)
Yohden Primary School, Peterlee

Candyland

C andy is my favourite thing at the shops
A te the chocolate bar
N o complaining about candy
D o eat candy every day, all day
Y ay, chocolate bars!
L ose salad, eat candy!
A t the shops, get candy and sweets
N o one likes salad, candy and sweets all the way
D o buy candies at the shops.

Sadie Bell (9)
Yohden Primary School, Peterlee

Candyland

C otton candy, the smell of my mouth,
A m I the only one who likes sweets?
N o one is as lucky as me,
D rumsticks melt in my mouth,
Y ellow chocolate-covered bananas,
L ollipop trees,
A nd sherbet sand,
N othing could be better than American candy,
D own in Candyland.

Sofia Bell May (9)
Yohden Primary School, Peterlee

Dinosaur Worry

The sun shone, then the moon,
But the sun came soon.
People are happy, some are sad,
But they might turn mad.
Dinosaurs were having a great time,
But escaping dinosaurs would be a crime.
The fire from the volcano,
Smelt like a busted tyre.
Children were playing,
But one was praying to the dinosaurs.

Thomas Wright (9)
Yohden Primary School, Peterlee

Football

F ootball is my most dreamed sport

O nly I could be the best.

O ff goes the football.

T errific goal!

B alls flying through the air.

A goal we scored.

L eaping, the ball went in the back of the net.

L asering it in the back of the net, I got Man of the Match.

Harley Storey (9)
Yohden Primary School, Peterlee

Dream Land

D ream and believe everything,
R oyalty rules the land,
E yes as beautiful as the ocean,
A rt is an expression of life,
M akeup, you don't need.

L ipstick smudges,
A re you having fun?
N ice people care,
D ancing in the moonlight.

Lily Wright (9)
Yohden Primary School, Peterlee

Football

F or tonight, I close my eyes,

O h, how I dream.

O f football and playing with my team,

T omorrow is the day I win the cup,

B ut for now, I rest,

A nd then the crowd roar,

L egs are ready to score a goal,

L oud, so loud, the crowd cheers my goal.

Harvey Robson (9)
Yohden Primary School, Peterlee

My Baby

My baby is sweet like sugar,
It's just like you no matter what you do,
I will be there,
Since I was one,
I dreamt upon the stars for you
My baby's name is Asha-May,
Now I am excited for you to come.

Ava Joan (8)
Yohden Primary School, Peterlee

YOUNG WRITERS INFORMATION

We hope you have enjoyed reading this book – and that you will continue to in the coming years.

If you're a young writer who enjoys reading and creative writing, or the parent of an enthusiastic poet or story writer, do visit our website **www.youngwriters.co.uk**. Here you will find free competitions, workshops and games, as well as recommended reads, a poetry glossary and our blog.

If you would like to order further copies of this book, or any of our other titles, then please give us a call or visit **www.youngwriters.co.uk**.

Young Writers
Remus House
Coltsfoot Drive
Peterborough
PE2 9BF
(01733) 890066
info@youngwriters.co.uk

 **YoungWritersUK**    **YoungWritersCW**
youngwriterscw    **youngwriterscw**